W9-DEG-268

SUPER**SCIENCE**
INFOGRAPHICS

THE SOLAR SYSTEM THROUGH INFOGRAPHICS

Nadia Higgins

graphics by
Lisa Waananen

Lerner Publications Company
Minneapolis

Lerner Publications Company
A division of Lerner Publishing Group, Inc.
241 First Avenue North
Minneapolis, MN U.S.A. 55401

Website address: www.lernerbooks.com

Main text set in Univers LT Std 12/15.
Typeface provided by Adobe Systems.

Library of Congress Cataloging-in-Publication Data

Higgins, Nadia.
    The solar system through infographics / by Nadia Higgins.
        p.   cm. — (Super science infographics)
    Includes index.
    ISBN 978–1–4677–1289–7 (lib. bdg. : alk. paper)
    ISBN 978–1–4677–1789–2 (eBook)
    1. Astronomy—Juvenile literature. 2. Solar system—Juvenile
literature. I. Title.
    QB46.H54 2014
    523.2—dc23   2013004838

Manufactured in the United States of America
1 – BP – 7/15/13

CONTENTS

A COSMIC ROLLER COASTER RIDE

Do you have a future in astronomy?
To find out, take this test.

1. Do you like mysteries?

2. Are you good at debating?

3. Are you cool with realizing that your ideas are basically wrong?

4. Can you read really big—really, really big—numbers?

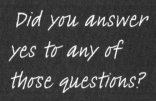

Did you answer yes to any of those questions?

CONGRATULATIONS!

You have what it takes to dive into the science of space. Astronomers will tell you, these days, it sure does feel like a roller coaster ride. Loads of data and new discoveries are turning old ideas upside-down. And they're raising even *more* questions. It could make you want to scream your head off in a mixture of fear and excitement.

Astronomers use graphs, charts, and other infographics to help sort through all the information. These graphics can make those big, mysterious ideas a bit clearer. Are you ready to join in the fun? Let's get started!

HOLY GALACTIC GAS BALLS!

Do you ever feel like a tiny speck in a vast, mysterious universe? Well, *you are.* Our visible universe is so huge that a beam of light—which could zip around Earth 7.5 times in a single second—would take 28 billion years to cross it. Check out some of the universe's other amazing stats:

OUR GALAXY

Our sun is just a blip among 400 billion other stars in our Milky Way Galaxy. These burning balls of gas come with half a trillion planets orbiting around them.

THE SUN

Imagine the sun was a bucket. You could dump one million Earths inside it.

THE VISIBLE UNIVERSE

Now, add in 100 billion more galaxies. And that's just what humans know about. The number of all the grains of sand on Earth isn't even close to how many stars are out there.

AND BEYOND . . .

Our universe is growing—and faster every day. Space is stretching out like pizza dough, pulling galaxies with it. Plus, who says ours is the only universe? What about a multiverse? Parallel universes could exist in dimensions outside of our known time or space. Wild!

ANDROMEDA

the closest spiral galaxy

2.2 million light-years

HOW FAR IS IT FROM EARTH?

SATURN

80 light minutes

PROXIMA CENTAURI

4.2 light-years

the closest star to the sun

SUN

8 light minutes

MOON

1.3 light seconds

Large distances in space are measured by how long light would take to travel from one point to another. For instance, a light-year is the distance light can travel in one year—nearly 6 million miles (9.5 million kilometers)!

OUTER SPACE IN EIGHT MIND-BLOWING STEPS

How did the universe begin? Follow the bouncing planet as it travels the timeline.

3 BILLION YEARS AFTER THE BIG BANG
Galaxies grow and pull together. Some giant stars collapse into black holes.

10 BILLION YEARS AGO

8 BILLION YEARS AGO:
Massive stars have been dying in huge explosions for several billion years by this point. These stars held elements that are necessary for life. Those elements continue spreading out across the universe.

7 BILLION YEARS AGO

14 BILLION YEARS AGO, GIVE OR TAKE . . . All matter, time, energy, and space is packed into an incredibly hot, dense, and tiny point.

. . . ONE SECOND AFTER THAT! The point has exploded into a 10 billion °F (5.6 billion °C) cloud of tiny bits of matter. This cloud is already universe-sized. Scientists call this event the big bang.

THE NEXT 500,000 YEARS: The whole thing keeps expanding. It also cools down. Hydrogen and helium gases begin to form. Space becomes see-through.

14 BILLION YEARS AGO

1 BILLION YEARS AFTER THE BIG BANG: Gravity continues pulling pockets of gas together. The very first stars and galaxies form.

12 BILLION YEARS AGO

5 BILLION YEARS AGO: Our sun is born inside the Milky Way. A disk of gas and dust around the sun begins to collapse into planets, moons, and asteroids.

4.5 BILLION YEARS AGO: Earth is in orbit and ready for action!

6 BILLION YEARS AGO

BIG BANG BREAKDOWN

No doubt, questions remain about the big bang theory. But most scientists agree on the basic event. How did they piece it all together? It's the typical science story: one good idea led to another.

BIG IDEA: The big bang produced radiation (waves of energy) that cooled as the universe expanded. These waves are known as cosmic microwave background (CMB).
DATE: 1948

GEORGE GAMOW
(1904–1968)
Russian-born American physicist

4

BIG IDEA: Proving Gamow's theory by detecting CMB.
DATE: 1965

ARNO A. PENZIAS (b. 1933)
ROBERT W. WILSON (b. 1936)
American physicists

5

BIG IDEA: The general theory of relativity, which redefined ideas of space, time, matter, energy, and gravity.

DATE: 1916

ALBERT EINSTEIN
(1879–1955)
German-born physicist

1

BIG IDEA: The universe is expanding in all directions and at predictable speeds, as if it was blasted from a single source.

DATE: 1920s

EDWIN HUBBLE
(1889–1953)
American astronomer

2

BIG IDEA: The universe began as a tiny, dense "super-atom."

DATE: 1920s

GEORGES LEMAÎTRE
(1894–1966)
Belgian astronomer

3

BIG IDEA: Detailed data on CMB. That data allowed scientists to piece together a timeline of the universe.

DATE: 1990–1992

NASA'S COBE SATELLITE
(launched 1989)

6

LIVES OF THE STARS

Stars are the universe's hottest real estate. These scorching balls of gas burn by joining atoms—tiny particles of matter—inside their cores. This is called nuclear fusion, and it creates incredible light and heat. That energy also fights gravity, so the star doesn't collapse.

Eventually, the star's fuel gets used up. As the star dies, it changes.

1 NEBULA
Stars are born in giant clouds of gas. Gravity pulls the gases into a ball that gets hotter and hotter.

2 GIANT OR SUPERGIANT STAR
A bigger star burns through its hydrogen fuel faster. It's so hot, it's blue.

2 MEDIUM-SIZED STAR (LIKE OUR SUN)
When the ball gets hot enough, hydrogen atoms begin to fuse (join). This action keeps the star going for billions of years.

3 RED GIANT
The star uses up its hydrogen fuel. Gravity crushes the star's core. The outer layers expand and cool, creating a giant red star. The biggest stars with the hottest cores are red supergiants.

THANKS FOR EVERYTHING, STARS!

Did you know that every single atom in your body, beside hydrogen, came from a star? During nuclear fusion, new elements are made. In most stars, hydrogen combines to form helium. Red supergiants are the universe's biggest element factories. They cook up most elements found in the universe. Amazing!

3 RED SUPERGIANT
Like a red giant, only bigger and with a hotter core.

4 SUPERNOVA
The red supergiant runs out of fuel. It collapses and explodes in an instant. This massive explosion can be as bright as 4 billion suns! The star's matter shoots into space. It ends up in nebulae that will form new stars and planets.

5 BLACK HOLE
If the star was big enough, the leftover particles collapse into an area of space called a black hole. Gravity is so strong in black holes, even light can't escape.

5 NEUTRON STAR
Leftover particles fuse into an incredibly dense ball. It's a tiny fraction of the size of Earth, but its mass could be three times our sun's!

4 WHITE DWARF
The outer layers have blown away. The core is cooling down.

5 BLACK DWARF
The star has cooled down so much that it's too faint to detect.

NEBULA

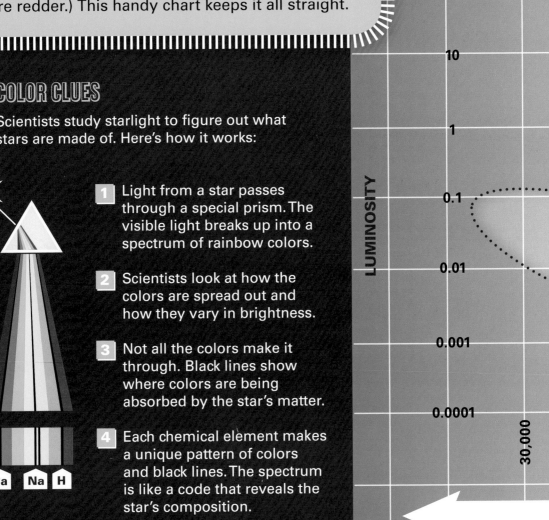

ALL KINDS OF TWINKLE

You don't have to be a rocket scientist to tell that some stars are easier to see than others. Still, scientists have made, well, a science out of showing star's differences. They measure five qualities: brightness (called luminosity), color, surface temperature, size, and mass. Those characteristics are all related. For example, color depends on surface temperature. (Cooler stars are redder.) This handy chart keeps it all straight.

COLOR CLUES

Scientists study starlight to figure out what stars are made of. Here's how it works:

1 Light from a star passes through a special prism. The visible light breaks up into a spectrum of rainbow colors.

2 Scientists look at how the colors are spread out and how they vary in brightness.

3 Not all the colors make it through. Black lines show where colors are being absorbed by the star's matter.

4 Each chemical element makes a unique pattern of colors and black lines. The spectrum is like a code that reveals the star's composition.

Ca Na H

100,000

10,000

1,000

100

10

1

0.1

0.01

0.001

0.0001

LUMINOSITY

30,000

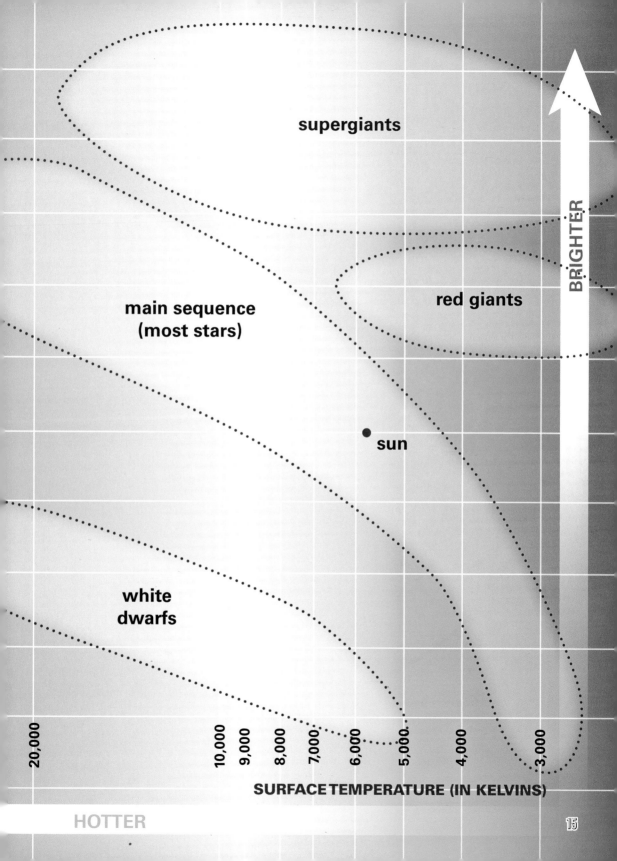

supergiants

main sequence
(most stars)

red giants

sun

white
dwarfs

BRIGHTER

20,000   10,000 9,000 8,000 7,000 6,000 5,000   4,000   3,000

SURFACE TEMPERATURE (IN KELVINS)

HOTTER

DOOMED!

Most black holes start with a supernova. The leftovers of a massive star collapse into a point that has mind-blowingly powerful gravity. Now, imagine space and time as a piece of stretchy fabric. The point dents that fabric, making a funnel shape. Space—and everything in it—rushes down the funnel like water going into a waterfall, only a gazillion times faster. Nothing, not even light, is fast enough to get out.

SINGULARITY
All mass gets sucked into here. This isn't a tiny ball. It's an infinitely small time-and-space warping point.

EVENT HORIZON
The boundary of the black hole. Once inside here, even light can't escape.

What would happen if you fell into a black hole? One thing's for sure—you're not climbing back out.

1. At first, you don't feel the black hole's gravity pulling on you. As you free-fall, you feel weightless.

2. Your feet start to feel weird. They're closer to the black hole than your head is. Gravity is pulling harder on them.

3. If you were rubber, you'd stretch way out. Instead, you snap in two. Your body halves get funneled toward the singularity.

4. Gravity gets even stronger. There's a LOT more snapping in two. Soon your body gets broken up into atoms, then atomic particles.

5. The atomic stuff that made you is gone. Not broken down or reshaped—gone. Luckily, it wasn't all for nothing. Your mass adds to the black hole's awesome sucking power!

SUN CAM

You really can't overstate the importance of the sun. First off, we'd all be dead without it. But did you know it contains *99.8 percent* of all the mass in our solar system? Check out some of the stuff that goes down on this awesome, life-giving star.

WHAT'S IT MADE OF?

Plasma, a superhot form of gas, makes up most of the sun. Most of that plasma is hydrogen.

72%
HYDROGEN

26%
HELIUM

2%
OTHER ELEMENTS
(oxygen, carbon, neon, nitrogen, magnesium, iron, silicon)

Electrically charged particles called protons and electrons constantly fly off the sun. This is called **SOLAR WIND**.

The **CORONA** is the highest part of the sun's atmosphere.

The lowest part of the sun's atmosphere, or **PHOTOSPHERE**, is what scientists mean by the sun's surface. It is about 10,000°F (5,500°C).

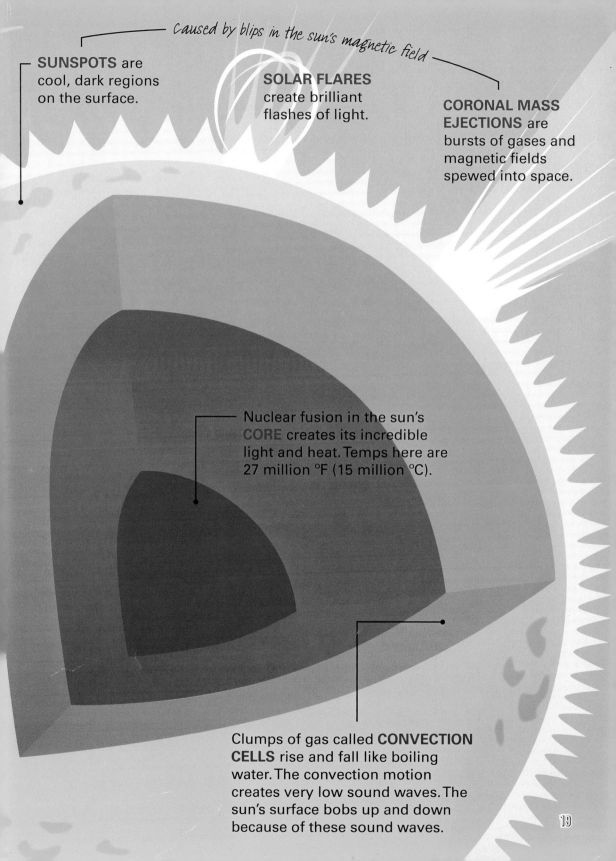

caused by blips in the sun's magnetic field

SUNSPOTS are cool, dark regions on the surface.

SOLAR FLARES create brilliant flashes of light.

CORONAL MASS EJECTIONS are bursts of gases and magnetic fields spewed into space.

Nuclear fusion in the sun's **CORE** creates its incredible light and heat. Temps here are 27 million °F (15 million °C).

Clumps of gas called **CONVECTION CELLS** rise and fall like boiling water. The convection motion creates very low sound waves. The sun's surface bobs up and down because of these sound waves.

19

PLANET FACT BLAST

Not just any giant orbiting ball can be a planet. In 2006 scientists at the International Astronomical Union (IAU) laid down some planetary rules. A planet a) must orbit the sun, b) must be round or almost, and c) can't share its orbit with a bunch of other objects.

Planets fall into two main groups. The four inner planets, including Earth, are terrestrial (rocky) planets. The four outer planets are huge gas giants. Take a look at how they all stack up.

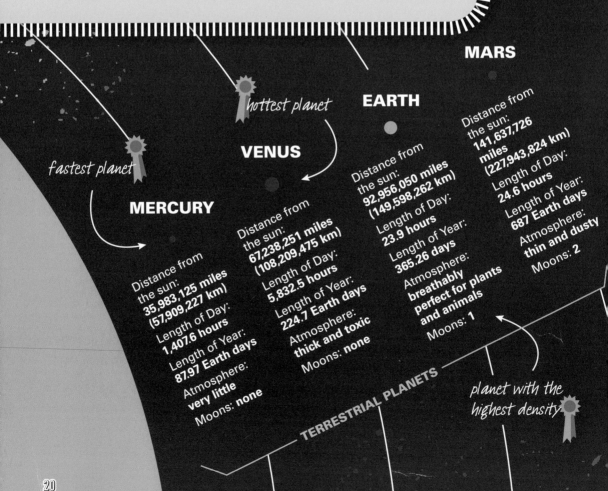

MARS

EARTH

hottest planet

VENUS

fastest planet

MERCURY

MERCURY

Distance from the sun:
35,983,125 miles (57,909,227 km)
Length of Day:
1,407.6 hours
Length of Year:
87.97 Earth days
Atmosphere:
very little
Moons: **none**

VENUS

Distance from the sun:
67,238,251 miles (108,209,475 km)
Length of Day:
5,832.5 hours
Length of Year:
224.7 Earth days
Atmosphere:
thick and toxic
Moons: **none**

EARTH

Distance from the sun:
92,956,050 miles (149,598,262 km)
Length of Day:
23.9 hours
Length of Year:
365.26 days
Atmosphere:
breathably perfect for plants and animals
Moons: **1**

MARS

Distance from the sun:
141,637,726 miles (227,943,824 km)
Length of Day:
24.6 hours
Length of Year:
687 Earth days
Atmosphere:
thin and dusty
Moons: **2**

planet with the highest density

TERRESTRIAL PLANETS

coldest planet

longest year

NEPTUNE

most tilted

URANUS

biggest planet

most moons

SATURN

Distance from the sun: **2,795,173,960 miles** (4,498,396,441 km)

Length of Day: **16.1 hours**

Length of Year: **59,800 Earth days**

Atmosphere: **incredibly deep with super fast winds**

Moons: **13**

Distance from the sun: **1,783,744,300 miles** (2,870,658,186 km)

Length of Day: **17.2 hours**

Length of Year: **30,589 Earth days**

Atmosphere: **looks blue from methane gas**

Moons: **27**

JUPITER

Distance from the sun: **886,489,416 miles** (1,426,666,422 km)

Length of Day: **10.7 hours**

Length of Year: **10,747 Earth days**

Atmosphere: **windy; bands of color**

Moons: **62**

Distance from the sun: **483,638,564 miles** (778,340,821 km)

Length of Day: **9.9 hours**

Length of Year: **4,331 Earth days**

Atmosphere: **stormy and windy; bands of color**

Moons: **66**

GAS GIANTS

WEIGH YOUR DOG

The more mass a planet has, the stronger its gravity. If your dog has a mass of 45 kilograms, he weighs 100 pounds here on Earth. How much would he weigh on other planets?

Mercury	**38 lbs (17 kg)**	
Venus	**91 lbs (41 kg)**	
Earth	**100 lbs (45 kg)**	
Mars	**38 lbs (17 kg)**	
Jupiter	**253 lbs (115 kg)**	
Saturn	**107 lbs (49 kg)**	
Uranus	**91 lbs (41 kg)**	
Neptune	**114 lbs (52 kg)**	

DON'T FORGET THE SMALL STUFF

Planets and stars get the most press. But space is full of other, smaller stuff you don't want to overlook. Let's break it down, from biggest to smallest.

BIGGEST

DWARF PLANETS
Like planets, these guys orbit the sun and are round. But they are smaller and they share their orbit paths. As of 2012, five dwarf planets have made the cut.

ASTEROIDS
Our solar system houses at least half a million of these giant, rocky space chunks. (Probably more.) Most of them orbit the sun inside the asteroid belt, between Mars and Jupiter.

COMETS
These space snowballs are each about the size of a small town. Comets orbit way out in the solar system. When they get close to the sun, they melt, spewing dust and gas, and look like a star with a tail.

SPACE JUNK
Even space has litter: Human-made stuff left over from past space missions. Think broken-down spacecraft, satellites, fuel jugs—even paint chips. How much is out there in Earth's orbit? NASA reports at least 21,000 pieces that are 4 inches (10 centimeters) or bigger!

METEORS
These are meteoroids that fall into a planet's atmosphere and burn up. Friction (rubbing) with the air makes them burn, leaving a trail of light we call a shooting star.

METEOROIDS
These rocks can be as small as a tiny grain or as big as a boulder. They orbit the sun along with whatever space object they broke off—except when they're crashing into stuff. When they fall to Earth's surface and don't burn up in the atmosphere, they are called meteorites.

ENTER THE DARK SIDE

What is the universe made of? The answer to this simple question has changed, big time, since the 1970s. Atoms—those microscopic units of matter that make up stars, planets, and us—are just a tiny part of what's out there.

3% ATOMS
Stuff we can see.

Hydrogen............75%	
Helium 24%	
Everything else....1%	

As for the ordinary part of the universe, it's mainly just hydrogen and helium. The rest of the elements all together make up just one hundredth of matter we can see.

27%

DARK MATTER
Mysterious matter that doesn't give off or take in light. Dark matter is everywhere—yes, even inside you this very minute. Scientists know about it only by measuring its gravity.

THEY CAN PROVE IT

Scientists know barely anything about dark matter and dark energy. How do they even know these exist?

DARK MATTER

1. Stars inside galaxies are moving way too fast for their mass. Gravity from dark matter must be pulling on them.

2. Galaxies inside clusters are also moving too fast, given their mass.

3. Scientists know that gravity bends light. But light coming from some distant galaxies is distorted by more gravity than ordinary matter could create.

DARK ENERGY

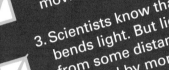

The big bang sent everything shooting away from other matter. By now, gravity should be slowing things down. Instead, the universe is expanding more quickly than ever.

70%

DARK ENERGY

This mysterious antigravity force is making the universe expand.

LOOK UP

On the next clear night, get a blanket, some binoculars, and find an outdoor spot away from city lights. Marvel at these top sights in North America's night sky.

THE MOON
See craters best on a crescent moon or a quarter moon, not a full moon.

TOTAL LUNAR ECLIPSE
The moon turns blood red as it passes through Earth's shadow. We get seven or so of these stunning shows per decade.

VENUS
Look toward the sun just before sunrise or after sunset to see the brightest planet.

PERSEID METEOR SHOWER

This beautiful light show peaks around August 12 every year. Expect sixty dazzling light streaks per hour if you watch during the peak time, from 2 to 5 A.M.

SCORPIUS

This constellation is best seen in July. It's easy to make out the scorpion's head, curved tail, and stinger, as well the reddish star, Antares, at its heart.

SIRIUS

This is the brightest star in our night sky. As it twinkles, it flickers with colors. Look for it on chilly winter nights.

JUPITER'S MOONS

Jupiter is a bright white dot, visible at night for much of the year. Use binoculars to see its four biggest moons near it.

HELLOOOOO?

Do your friends make fun of you for believing in aliens? Just tell them you're an astrobiologist. These scientists study the possibility of alien life. In 1961 astrobiologist Frank Drake came up with an equation for measuring intelligent life in our galaxy. Modern scientists estimate that our galaxy hosts as many as 20 *billion* Earth-like planets.

DO THE MATH

The Drake Equation is really just a tool. There's no single right answer. Still, playing around with it is fun.

Scientists have some idea what these values are.

$$N = R^* \times f_p \times n_e$$

Number of advanced civilizations that humans could detect (most likely, through radio telescopes). Drake's answer was 10,000.

Rate of how many stars are born per year in our galaxy

Fraction of stars that have planets. (Remember that a fraction is a number less than one.)

Average number of planets in a solar system that could support life

LIFE CLOSE TO HOME

Does life exist in our solar system? If so, it's microscopic. Scientists have their eyes on three likely candidates.

 1 Under the surface of Mars, likely in a hidden source of water

2 Inside oceans under the frozen surface of Europa, one of Jupiter's moons

3 Inside liquid hydrocarbon lakes on Saturn's moon Titan

This is all multiplication. If any of these numbers equals zero, the whole thing goes bust.

$$\times f_l \times f_i \times f_c \times L$$

 Fraction of those planets on which life actually begins

 Fraction of life-forms that develop intelligence

 Fraction of intelligent life that develops civilizations with satellites and other transmitters, like we have

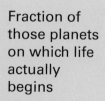 How long those civilizations send out signals we could detect

Your guess is as good as any.

Glossary

ASTEROID: huge chunk of rock that orbits the sun. Many orbit between Mars and Jupiter.

ATOM: a microscopic unit of matter. An atom contains electrically charged bits called protons and electrons.

BIG BANG: the theory that the universe began as a tiny point of incredibly dense matter about 14 billion years ago

BLACK HOLE: an area in space that has such strong gravity, even light can't get out

COMET: a dusty chunk of ice that orbits the sun way out in the solar system

DWARF PLANET: a round body, smaller than a planet, that orbits the sun. Dwarf planets don't have enough gravity to clear their orbits, so they move through the solar system with other objects.

ELEMENT: a substance, such as oxygen or iron, that is made of one kind of atom only. Stars make elements through nuclear fusion.

GRAVITY: a force that pulls objects toward one another. Gravity makes stars form and keeps planets in orbit.

HYDROGEN: the lightest chemical element. Most of the atomic universe is made of hydrogen.

MASS: a property of matter that determines how much gravity it has

METEOR: a meteoroid that falls into a planet's atmosphere and burns up. It gives off a streak of light as it burns in the sky.

METEOROID: a small chunk of space rock or metal hurtling through the solar system

NEBULA: a huge cloud of spinning gas from which stars and planets form

NUCLEAR FUSION: the process by which atoms smash into one another and combine to form new elements

PLANET: a round body that orbits the sun. A planet is big enough so that its gravity clears its orbital path.

PLASMA: a state of matter like extremely hot gas that is sensitive to magnetism. The sun is mostly hydrogen plasma.

RADIATION: energy, such as light, that comes out from an object in the form of waves or particles

SUPERNOVA: a massive explosion at the end of the life of a red supergiant. A supernova scatters chemical elements throughout the universe.

Aguilar, David A. *13 Planets: The Latest View of the Solar System.* Washington, DC: National Geographic Kids, 2011.
That's right, thirteen planets: eight classical planets and five dwarf ones. This clear, fact-packed book makes you rethink what you know about the solar system.

Croswell, Ken. *The Lives of Stars.* Honesdale, PA: Boyds Mill Press, 2009.
Written by an astronomer with a Ph.D., this book for kids gets down to the nitty-gritty.

DeCristofano, Carolyn Cinami. *A Black Hole Is Not a Hole.* Watertown, MA: Charlesbridge Publishing, 2012.
This is a fun, in-depth look at one of the most mind-blowing topics in astronomy today.

Fullman, Joe, Ian Graham, Sally Regan, and Isabel Thomas. *Look Now: The World in Facts, Stats, and Graphics.* New York: DK Publishing, 2010.
This infographic extravaganza has enough facts to power your brain for years.

Kids Discover: Infographics
http://www.kidsdiscover.com/blog/?tab=infographics
This site proves that any topic can make a good infographic. Check out "10 Super Fun Ways to Make Summer Last," as well as "Solar Eclipse" and "How the *Titanic* Sank."

NASA Kids' Club
http://www.nasa.gov/audience/forkids/kidsclub/flash/index.html
This is THE site for outer space games, photos, and facts.

National Geographic Kids: Science and Space Videos
http://video.nationalgeographic.com/video/kids/science-space-kids
Check out restored footage from the 1969 moon landing, concept animation of future NASA projects, and more on this cool site.

The Planetary Society: For Kids
http://www.planetary.org/explore/for-kids
This site has great activities, experiments, and facts. Its best resource, though, are archived episodes of "Consider the Following," with Bill Nye, the Science Guy. Find out how scientists find new planets, how spacecraft handle extreme temperatures, and more.

Space: A Visual Encyclopedia. New York: DK Publishing, 2010.
This beautiful book covers just about every space angle you can think of. Use it as a diving-off point for deeper investigations.

Vogt, Gregory L. *Meteors and Comets.* Minneapolis, Lerner Publications, 2010.
What's the difference between a meteor and a comet? Hint: one's a chunk of metal and one's a chunk of ice. Pick up this book for tons more info on the small stuff in our solar system.

Index

PHOTO ACKNOWLEDGMENTS

Additional images in this book are used with the permission of: AIP Emilio Segre Visual Archives, Physics Today Collection, p. 10 (top); AIP Emilio Segre Visual Archives, p. 10 (bottom); the Illustrated London News, p. 11 (top); Courtesy of the Archives, California Institute of Technology, p. 11 (left); Hale Observatories, courtesy AIP Emilio Segre Visual Archives, p. 11 (right); NASA/COBE Science Team, p. 11 (bottom).